Disclaimer

All the information in this book is to be used for informational and educational purposes only. The author will not account in any way for any results that stem from the use of the contents herein. While conscious and creative attempts have been made to ensure that all information provided herein is as accurate and useful as possible, the author is not legally bound to be responsible for any damage caused by the accuracy as well as use/misuse of this information.

Contents

Contents

Introduction

Up until my second year in high school I'd been the sweet, naïve girl that always tried to do the right thing and always ended up getting hurt or betrayed. My self-esteem was low, every comment about me would affect me and I felt like I could never fit in. I got no attention from guys and even worse, some would bully me for being awkward and not looking conventionally attractive. Over the summer I've decided to make a change. I was done getting bullied so I got a few nice outfits and started using some makeup. I also decided to speak up for myself if they'd try to harass me and not just ignore them in the hopes that they'd go away. School started again and I could not believe how differently I was being treated. It's like the year before never even happened. The very same bullies were asking me on dates.

I made a few friends throughout high school and even though my looks and personality didn't change a lot, guys would always ask me out. Not only one type of guys, it was ranging from charismatic jocks to introverted nerds and geeks. Now, I could not really understand why. There were girls way prettier than me, but still I was the one receiving poems and flowers from the more romantic guys even though I never expressed interest in any of them. This also caused some girls to resent me even though I wasn't even interacting with these guy more than maybe having a casual conversation once every few days. This also led to people being very curious about whom and if I was talking to someone, even though other girls had boyfriends and caused drama. Why me out of everyone else? I could not escape this spotlight and I tried to be very private about everything.

I never thought too much of all of this, until I started to learn about manipulation and dark psychology. I read every book there was, I attended courses and fundamentally understood the human nature. Why were they so obsessed with everything I was doing? Why me and not anyone else? I finally understood what I did back then so that made people obsess over me.

And now I'm here to share the secrets of everything I've learned. You can apply everything in real life and be the most desired woman there is. I became the confident, seductive woman I am today. I can literally get any guy to do anything for me and soon you will too.

This book contains everything on how to become a seductive femme, how to induce obsession and how to be an undetectable manipulator. The terms and language used is very straightforward and might hurt your feelings, but this knowledge will make you incredibly powerful. This book is not only to learn about manipulation, but also to protect yourself against it as it is extremely common and being a victim of obsession is painful and hard to recover form.

Please do not share this knowledge with anyone, gatekeep it from men especially as this knowledge can be devastating in the wrong hands.

Word of advice: choose your victims carefully. Manipulating a person can be dangerous if you don't know when to stop as obsession breeds stalkers.

Chapter One

Manipulation 101

Before we explore the feminine types and start working on our rebirth as a femme fatale, we must learn the ins and outs of manipulation. It is important to intercept manipulation technics from the possible targets.

I've learned from a young age that a lot of men learn manipulation tactics and use them consciously. Granted, some choose not to use them but they still know about them. They don't even label it as manipulation, they're labeling it as "useful advice" on how to get women to like them. This is why I think it's important to learn about these techniques and notice possible patterns.

What is manipulation?
When people hear the term, they instantly think of some evil Wall Street-looking guy in a suit who's lying and deceiving everyone on a daily basis.

In reality, all of us have practiced manipulation at one point in our lives. Most likely without even realizing it. Manipulation is used in every aspect of our lives and mostly in our relationships.

There are a lot of manipulation techniques, but I've compiled the most common ones used. There are many variations,of these techniques, but the end goal of manipulation techniques remains the same and we will explore it shortly.

Manipulation Techniques

There are a lot of manipulation techniques, but I've compiled the most common ones used. There are many variations, but the end goal of manipulation techniques remains the same and we will explore it shortly.

The most common form of manipulation? Words not matching actions.

If a guy tells you he loves you but doesn't talk to you for days in a row or only hits you up at night – you're being manipulated.

He says he's sorry but does the same thing again? – Manipulation 101

Let's go over some terms:

- Love bombing - it's when he is overly attentive and affectionate at the beginning of a relationship, tries to make you feel special even though you haven't even started to bond yet

Example: he might say very early on that he loves you, that you're his soulmate and pitch you images of a future together. They force you into committing to them early – that way you're easier to manipulate.

- Gaslighting – he tries to deny his abusive actions by telling you it never happened, making you doubt reality and your own sanity. Might call you sensitive or overdramatic for reaction to abuse.

Some take it so far that you show them evidence of their behavior and they're still denying it.

Example:

- Guilt Tripping – he tries to use guilt as a way to emotionally blackmail you. A common example is when a guy starts crying right after being caught cheating. He tries to spin this narrative and paint himself as a victim of the circumstance.

Other examples: he threatens to harm himself if you leave him, he uses phrase like "If you'd actually love me/care, you would do this".

- Stonewalling – he refuses to have any type of communication, he stops responding and doesn't address any issue you bring up.

Common example: If he's given an ultimatum, he refuses to choose in the hopes that you forget about it and move on.

- Bread crumbing : He leads you on with romantic messages just enough to keep you interested. Conversation is very generic and shallow otherwise.
He always manages to phrase things in a way that gives you hope without committing himself to anything.

Example: He doesn't respond to your Whatsapp, but then he like your Instagram post, or you see they've watched your story. That keeps them on your radar and prevents you from moving on or forgetting about them.

- Not My Type: He purposefully follows and likes the pictures of girls that look completely different than you. He's trying to make you insecure and feel the need to prove yourself to him.

- Hot and Cold Method– the most common technique used and taught in every dark psychology course for men. In the 'hot' phase, you feel attention and attraction and it can feel intense. Especially if the love-bombing worked. Then comes the 'cold' phase when he pulls away, making you crave his attention and yearn for him. As a result, it leaves you feeling rejected, confused, frustrated.

The trick here is that by withdrawing his attention from you, your brain will start craving consistency. And once he comes around again, your brain will release dopamine. And so begins a literal addiction, as your brain will now recognize him as a source of pleasure.

- Projection This technique is also very popular today. There are many variations of it, but we'll stick to the most used one. To put it simple, they're accusing you of something they're actually doing. Does he suddenly start accusing you of cheating when you never gave him a reason to think that? He might be the one doing it and this creates paranoia. He's cheating and you probably know it so you're cheating back, right? Their guilt transforms into projection.

End Goal of Manipulation

What is the end goal of all these manipulation tactics? What are they trying to gain?

It's a power dynamic and the end goal of every type of manipulation in a relationship or in the dating stage is: <u>they're trying to make you chase them</u>. If they get you to do that, they know they can get away with a lot more.

That is why you see everyone saying "don't chase" - basically meaning don't respond to manipulation.

Here's how being manipulated feels like:

- You feel fear, obligation, guilt
- Relationship is very emotionally intense
- There is no consistency, they ghost you alot
- You feel confused, insecure, frustrated
- Your instincts tell you something is wrong

Don't think that all chemistries and commonalities are manipulations. You would lose your spontaneity and not everything is a game.
But at the same time, always reserve final judgment until you see concrete proof.

Now that you have an idea of what manipulation looks like and how to spot it, we will proceed to learn about the feminine types and how to harness your natural power. By doing this, you will naturally reject all manipulation attempts and only attract the best partners.

You will soon master the secret to becoming a powerful seductress and learn how get anyone and anything you want.

Chapter Two

The Inner Feminine

It is necessary for you to settle on a feminine type before you can even begin the process of finding a male target or reinventing yourself. Your road toward self-love must start with establishing a connection to the beautiful femininity you already possess. In addition, contrary to what is often believed, femininity does not entail that everything must be pink, soft, and airy.

The dark and light feminine are the two types of femininity that are often considered the most significant. Because it is mainly intended for femme fatal, vixens, and sirens, this book will place its primary emphasis on the dark feminine energy.

We will be concentrating on how to harness the power of the dark feminine energy and make it work for you to get anyone and everything you want.

A significant number of women make the conscious decision only to acknowledge the light side of their femininity while actively working to repress their darker side of femininity.

They don't allow themselves to feel these emotions because they've been conditioned to believe that the ability to seduce and manipulate are "masculine" qualities.

In addition, there are certain women who are entirely subservient to their dark femininity, which causes them to become its target and allows it to consume them. Dark feminine energy that has not been controlled is very harmful and may result in serious emotional, sexual, and physical issues.

It may also result in an inability to tap into light feminine characteristics such as a caring, empathetic, or loving behavior.

The challenge is to tap into your dark femininity and gain mastery over it without allowing it to take command of your life. Numerous sources regularly bring up dark femininity, but they never investigate its potential dangers or even attempt to explain the full scope of its effects. This book will equip you with the skills you need to channel the Dark Feminine, a potent force you must understand before you can channel it completely.

What Is Dark Feminine Energy?

The dark feminine is one-half of the divine feminine. She is not the negative aspect of the feminine but rather the dark, fiery, transformational, shadow aspect of womanhood.

Femininity and feminine energy often have negative and weak connotations because of how the patriarchy has shallowly defined femininity over the years. But this definition of femininity —fragile, passive, gentle, overly-receptive, obedient, quiet, a sexual object of desire, submitting to the masculine—is actually toxic femininity. This is not a true representation of the feminine.

Dark feminine energy refers to the harmful patterns that form when we conceal unpleasant feelings such as shame, remorse, and rage. This aspect of femininity is sometimes referred to as the "shadow side" of femininity. It should not be thought of as a distinct entity from the divine feminine energy since it is, at its core, the same thing.

Dark Feminine Traits:

·Mysterious

·Passionate

·Seductive

·Fearless

·Powerful

·Devilish

·Magnetic

·Manipulative

Although this is not always the case, we are predisposed to link darkness with a negative connotation. Through this energy, we may get a deeper appreciation for the mysteries of females, such as seduction, reproduction, death, and birth.

Everything has both positive and negative forms of energy. Just consider how the yin and the yang work together to keep the universe in equilibrium and balance. This is how harmony is maintained throughout the cosmos. There is always some evil to be found in the good. Some light, even in the darkest places, and the same is true of light and dark feminine energy. We must acknowledge and accept both the good and the dark sides of our personalities. The most effective step you can take is to accept and embrace everything.

Dark Feminine Goddesses

The Dark Feminine has been explored for centuries and has been a concept ever since the beginning of time.

Dark Feminine Goddesses

·Lilith
·Kali
·Circe
·Nyx

Dark Feminine Stars

·Alexa Demie
·Angelina Jolie
·Megan Foxx
·Monica Bellucci

These women embody the Dark Feminine to perfection. My favorite is our queen Alexa Demie. She is very magnetic and she keeps us wanting more of her because she's very private. That way she's maintaining the mystery around her and controlling the narrative.

Wounded Feminine

Before we learn how to access the Dark Feminine Energy, we must learn about the Wounded Feminine. We've all been in our wounded feminine state at some point. This stage usually occurs when you're young and you're trying to find yourself. Most likely in high school, but some women never grow out of this state. Unfortunately this is also when you're the most susceptible to manipulation.

Dark Feminine Energy helps us heal when we're in our Wounded Feminine state.

How to know you're still in your Wounded Feminine State

Checkbox

You:

Compete for male attention

Focus on other women's flaws to feel superior

Don't trust your intuition

Feel like you're constantly the victim

Feel jealous and bitter

Seek external validation

Find it hard to say no/weak boundaries

Lack of control over your emotions, have no emotional discipline

Attempted to manipulate someone but it backfires as you lack mental strength

How to Access the Dark Feminine Energy Within

Putting effort into bettering yourself in any manner requires both time and commitment.

In addition, no one strategy is successful for all. Reestablishing a connection with your inner self and unlearning destructive habits of thinking and action may be challenging, but the result is well worth the effort. Experiment with a couple of these strategies, see what works best for you, and discover the hidden feminine strength that lies dormant within you.

l. Shadow Work: When you do shadow work, it's helpful to imagine the mirror as a microscope. Consider the shadow self to be the dark and disowned aspects of our personalities that significantly influence our anxieties and negative thinking patterns.

Investigating your responses, presuppositions, ideas, and feelings may provide invaluable insight into your character's darker aspects. In most cases, times of extreme stress or strong emotion provide wonderful chances for one's self-discovery.

2. Meditation: Meditation is essential for accessing your dark feminine energy since it is such a strong technique that helps improve the link between the mind and the body.

By establishing a connection between your mind and body and purging poisonous, ego-driven ideas, you may allow the suppressed shadow version of yourself to emerge.

Do not pass judgment or criticism; rather, make room in your life for your uncertainties and concerns, and observe how these feelings gradually fade as you grow to know and comprehend them.

3. Practice self-love: Imagine that your shadow self is a younger sister or a friend who is lonely and confused and that they are you in this role.

Unfortunately, individuals can have more empathy for other people than for themselves; therefore, this frequently enables us to be nicer to ourselves. Combat this propensity by regularly engaging in rigorous self-love practices, such as reciting affirmations, keeping a diary, or scheduling days dedicated to self-care. The ways in which individuals choose to engage in self-love practices take on a variety of forms. Embrace emotional maturity by extending an olive branch to the part of yourself that you have suppressed in the past, and in the process, you will become unstoppable.

The Benefits of the Dark Feminine

As mentioned before, Dark Feminine helps us heal when we're at our worst. Some of us channel it without even realizing. After a breakup, a betrayal or a painful lesson, we realize it's time to evolve.

The Dark Feminine inside takes over and reestablishes strong boundaries and self-esteem.

Our spiritual development is hindered when we suppress a portion of who we are as individuals. Whether or not we are willing to acknowledge it, it is something that every one of us has engaged in at some point. Since childhood, we subconsciously push away aspects of ourselves with such force that we are blind to the degree to which we are clinging to those aspects.

We stubbornly disregard these features or attributes that society deems to be undesirable, and as a result, we cannot see the deep insight inside them.

Dark femininity is a source of a great deal of creative, sexual, and sensual energy for women, and those who are in touch with it feel it in abundance.

When you tap into this aspect of yourself, you will release the capacity to devour and conquer male energy, which will cause men to fall at your feet. You will also have the confidence to do so. It's almost like a type of alchemy, and it's something that all women have access to, but very few know anything about.

When we recognize, accept, and embrace the feminine aspect of our shadow self, our soul is able to mature to a deeper level. It may be difficult to reintegrate those aspects of yourself that you have spent so much time rejecting and pushing away, particularly when our egos struggle with every fiber of their being to maintain the status quo. However, mastering the power of one's dark femininity and becoming harmonious with oneself is a tremendously empowering endeavor. Having a positive connection with the dark feminine energy inside you is essential. We are indoctrinated from a young age with the idea that our divine/light femininity is the only quality that can make us appealing and desirable.

The lessons society teaches us tell us that we shouldn't give in to our feelings, shouldn't be too sexual, and shouldn't be too strong. However, this unfavorable conception of the dark feminine energy couldn't be farther from the reality of the situation. The capabilities of our dark femininity are equally as impressive as those of our light femininity.

At its worst, "black feminine energy" alludes to narcissistic inclinations toward manipulating other people, showing malice, and having an imbalance in their sexual lives. Although these characteristics are not in the least bit desirable, it is interesting to deepen our comprehension of the factors that inherently lead us to engage in certain activities.

Be careful not to let your darker self control you, but listen carefully to the advice that she has to offer. The strength that comes from embracing the power of dark feminine energy wholeheartedly is unmistakable. Our creative potential, sensuality, and passion are amplified when we delve into the dark side of our feminine nature. It requires bravery and patience, but the result is well worth the effort.

What is preventing you from uncovering the many facets of the feminine energy you possess?

Chapter Three

Reinventing the

Femme Fatale Persona

After discovering and connecting with our dark feminine energy and the necessity of looking into our shadow selves and embracing what we find, the next stage is to reinvent yourself and accept your inner femme fatale.

The term "femme fatale," refers to an alluring woman who is cunning, somewhat malevolent, and shrouded in mystery. Dark glitz is the quintessential representation of the femme fatale; she is alluring, intriguing, and sophisticated. The question remains, however, what produces the femme fatale?

What is the Femme Fatale Persona?

First, let's talk about the characteristics of a typical femme fatale. How she acts, how she thinks, and how you might adopt her ways of thinking and behavior to become more like her.

The femme fatale personality embodies **allure, mystery**, and **power** equally. People think of women like these as dangerous seductresses skilled at getting what they want. She is self-assured, in command of her environment, and adept at manipulating others around her to accomplish her goals. She knows how to **seduce, manipulate** and **destroy**.

The Femme Fatale is not one to shrink from danger, which is something that may work in both her favor and to her detriment.

On one hand, she is capable of having a vibrant and exciting personality, but on the other hand, she is also capable of being irresponsible and careless. Her tendency toward impulsivity puts her at risk of getting herself into precarious circumstances that she cannot effectively manage.

The femme fatale is constantly conscious of how her actions affect other people and uses her sexuality as a tactical advantage. The power of a woman to exert control over men without placing herself in danger is exemplified by the femme fatale archetype.

A fundamental aspect of this archetype is the femme fatale's ability to seduce powerful men with wealth and influence. Yet, she is not searching for a comfortable suburban house or the joys of a traditional family life.

Facets of a Femme Fatale Persona

The Femme Fatale archetype encompasses a wide range of character traits. Some of the most typical personas are as follows:

1. The Black Widow: A person with the Black Widow personality is very clever and manipulative. In most cases, they are charming and seductive, and as a result, they can effortlessly acquire what they want from other people. These people often have a shadowy and enigmatic side, which can be both fascinating and lethal.

2. The Flirt: A person with the flirt personality trait is someone who adores having fun and takes pleasure in the company of others. They tend to be highly gregarious individuals who enjoy being the life of the party. They are always looking for new and interesting ways to make other people laugh and have a good time. Flirts are typically upbeat and optimistic individuals who look for the best in others.

They are often strong believers in the saying, "live and let live," whether consciously or unconsciously, which means that they think everyone should be happy and enjoy life to the fullest extent possible. They can be very charming and understand precisely what it takes to make other people feel good about themselves. Flirts might sometimes come off as a little bit too over-the-top or theatrical, but that's how they like to have fun! In the end, all they want is for everyone to be satisfied.

3. The Circe: The goddess who worked enchantments is called Circe in Greek mythology, whence the name Circe originates. People whose personalities align with the Circe archetype are imaginative, contemplative, and outspoken. They often exhibit a deep appreciation for the visual arts, musical compositions, or written works. People that identify with the Circe archetype are usually gentle, empathetic, and concerned with maintaining harmonious relationships. They will often go out of their way to avoid confrontation and struggle with being aggressive and speaking up for themselves. However, they are often incredibly perceptive individuals who are able to provide profound insights into the lives and circumstances of other people. If you know someone with the Circe personality type, chances are you also know someone who is very gifted and highly insightful.

4. The Siren: A person with the siren personality exudes an abundance of charisma and charm. They have the power to make other people feel good, which they utilize to their advantage to control others around them. They tend to be very self-centered and care solely about themselves. They also tend to be sexually promiscuous and may have personalities that are highly addicting.

5. The Seductress: This kind of person has a reputation for being very self-assured and always ready to take control; they are aware of what they want and pursue it without making any apologies for their actions. There is much more to this personality type than meets the eye, despite the fact that some people may consider the seductress as deceptive or even as someone who uses their sexuality to achieve what they want. Seductresses are often bright, perceptive, and capable of displaying a high level of compassion when they choose.

Femme Fatale Character Traits

Emotional Embracement: For women to be strong, they do not need to give up their femininity or engage in behaviors that are harmful to themselves.

The femme fatale is a perfect symbol of the power of femininity. She is also the ideal metaphor for the absolute potential and darker side of the feminine's power.

A femme fatale is neither the "Great Mother" nor the "Terrible Mother" described by Carl Jung; rather, she is somewhere between these two extremes. She brings to our attention that whatever has the power to **create** can also **destroy**.

Unapologetically Confident: Her attitude is not hostile nor menacing in any way. This woman exudes an air of self-assurance. She is well aware of her capabilities and has devised a strategy for accomplishing her objectives, both of which relate to the goals and aspirations she has set for herself.

Passionate & Emotional: A femme fatale has the character trait of being passionate, energetic, and even overpowering at times. They may also experience rapid outbursts of rage or sadness. Because of the intensity with which they feel things, they are capable of becoming both excellent friends and strong opponents.

<u>Manipulative</u>: When it comes to achieving what they want, a femme fatale may be extremely charming and seductive when they need to be, but when it comes to getting what they want, they can also be very ruthless and cold. They often have a strong ability to read other people and manipulate the feelings of others to persuade them to do what they want. They are often quite skilled at concealing their own goals and objectives, and when they put their minds to it, they are capable of producing very compelling arguments. They are often skilled liars and manipulators who have the ability to provide arguments that are quite persuasive. They are willing to hurt others or take advantage of others to achieve what they want, and they will do whatever it takes to get it.

Chapter Four

Investing In Your Femme Fatale

To improve your life and prospects for the future, you must "invest" in yourself by devoting time, energy, and money to these ends. This is a crucial stage in the evolution of the femme fatale. Women often make unintentional investments in the people around us, particularly the males with whom we have relationships. This is not always a negative trait but may lead to overcompensation, dependence, and neediness.

When you look the part of a femme fatale, you have no choice but to play the part as well. It is common knowledge that Femme Fatales can mesmerize and control the men they encounter. The question now is, how does one become a femme fatale?

Creating the Mystery

Remember when I was told you that in high school guys were constantly asking me on dates and people were always curious about me? The reason behind it was because I was unconsciously creating an **aura of mystery**. I'll present to you my favorite quote from the 48 Laws of Power by Robert Greene:

"People are enthralled by mystery; because it invites constant interpretation, they never tire of it.
The mysterious cannot be grasped. And what cannot be seized and consumed creates power."

People will often find themselves thinking of you and they'll unconsciously try to figure you out. As they won't find out much about you, they're minds will come up with scenarios and fantasies and will try to approach you.

Tips on creating the aura of mystery

Post less on social media – if you have a habit of posting daily start by reducing it to 2-3 time per week.

Show more **layers of yourself.** If you're mostly in your dark feminine energy, show light feminine traits every once in a while. For instance, if someone is having a bad day, show a gentle and compassionate side, give them advice and assure them it's going to be alright. If you're a light femme, show a **glimmer of darkness** every once in a while. This creates uncertainty and will make them crave for more.

Never make statements about yourself aka never brag! Let your actions control the narrative. And make it seem like everything you do is effortless.

The fascination of the femme fatale lies precisely in the fact that she remains a mystery. As human beings, our brains want a sense of certainty and consistency. As a result, whenever we are confronted with anything that cannot be evaluated to its full extent, our brains go into overdrive attempting to comprehend it. Because of this, maintaining an air of mystery is beneficial; it is one of the factors that causes others to get infatuated with you, at which point their imaginations begin to go amok. Make it a challenge for others to discover things about you; if you give out too much information, you won't have any mystique left. Remaining mysterious also protects you and your reputation, as everyhting you say and do can be used against you by people who are trying to take you down.

Don't air all of your grievances publicly, even if you're having a particularly challenging day. Learn to have a strong inner strength as well as a strong will.

Raw Sexual Magnetism

Becoming magnetic and developing sex appeal is the most important step for a femme fatale.

This has little to do with looks, despite what many people believe. The trick is to **feel connected to your body and embrace your sexuality.** We actually do this when we tap into our **dark feminine energy.**

How to develop
sexual magnetism

Connect to your body

Love and celebrate your body. Get comfortable in your skin and examine yourself naked in the mirror. Put on a Cardi B song and dance to it. Embrace the baddie inside of you.

Use these powerful affirmations everytime you look in the mirror:

I love how beautiful my body is

I ooze sex appeal

I am irresitable

I am sexual

I am the baddest

My body is perfect

How to develop
sexual magnetism

Body Language

There are tons of body language tricks on TikTok and Social Media but let's get down to the nitty-gritty, need-to-know basics — eye contact along with head and back posture. Without staring, make sure you're giving eye contact during key moments of conversation. Let your instincts guide you.

Keep your back straight and your chin slightly angled down. This conveys confidence without seeming haughty, making them irresistibly attracted to you.

How to develop

sexual magnetism

Show off your assets

We all have a body part that we're proud of whether it's the back, legs, waist, bum.
Whatever body part you love the most, show it off. Since you're confident about that specific body part, you'll enjoy showing it off which brings out your sex appeal.

Self-care and wellbeing

Cut out insecure people

I know it sounds harsh, but these people will bring you down. Most of the time their insecurities run deep and unless they actively try to work on themselves, they cannot be helped.

They'll just secretly resent you and you'll feel uncomfortable being your gorgeous self around them. Keeping insecure people around might end up in a huge betrayal just like in Maddy and Cassie's case on Euphoria. Same goes for toxic people and manipulators. That way you make room for high quality people to enter your life.

Self-care and wellbeing

Exercise

Yoga, Pilates, Gym or even just dancing – make sure to move your body. Any type of exercise is beneficial for both your physical and mental health. It literally changes your mood.

Invest in Skincare

Develop a skin care routine. Make sure to always use SPF daily and a good moisturizer depending on your skin type!

Invest in Knowledge

Buy self-help books to improve yourself and the areas you want to work on.
Here are some recommendations:

Manipulation – The 48 Laws of Power
Productivity – Atomic Habits
Influence – How to win friends and influence people
Self- help - The Subtle Art of Not Giving a F*ck

Appearance

As stated many time before, what makes you magnetic is your energy and how you perceive yourself. The way you see yourself is how others will see you as well. Many gorgeous and conventionally attractive women today are subjected to inhumane treatment by males because they are unaware of the power that women possess. There are also women who, at first look, seem "ordinary" or unconventionally gorgeous but have men figuratively wrapped around their finger because of their charm.

The trick is not to look like a certain someone, but to look like the best version of yourself. Choose a style that defines you and use makeup that suits your facial features.

Make-up

Everything is cyclical so the fashion trends will always change and so will the makeup styles. I've tried them all: the clean girl aesthetic (makes me look sweaty), the no-makeup makeup, the rockstar girlfriend makeup and while some worked, there is one makeup style that never fails anyone.

I've literally not seen anyone not look absolutely enchanting with it.

It's being rebranded every year, but it's the **siren eyes makeup** (ex fox eyes, ex cat eyes)
This works absolutely amazing on anyone and you'll look hypnotizing when making eye contact with anyone.

Clothing

I recommend taking the **Kibbe Body Type** test to determine your body shape and build your wardrobe around it.
It was a game changer for me.
Also, use clothing items that accentuate your best features and your curves. Wear whatever you feel most confident in.
To not over-do it, you need a way to balance looking sexy and classy at the same time – **the upper-lower contrast**. If you wear something more showy on top, you can balance it out with something more modest on the bottom and vice versa.

Affirmations

Affirmations change your mentality to one of thankfulness, positivism, and confidence. They are essential components of many universal rules, but they are also personal. They have the potential to act as a source of encouragement, eliminate negativity, create structure, and assist in the development of a certain attitude, in this particular instance, developing the femme fatale mentality.

These affirmations help you shift your perception of yourself and make a quantum leap towards being the finest possible version of who you are. The most important step in being a seductive and alluring femme fatale is cultivating a sense of sexuality and self-assurance.

You will be able to train your subconsciousness to think that you are these things (which you are.) Therefore, you repeat these affirmations until you believe them and you will step into a reality where you are the ultimate seductress.

- I am protected by the divine
- People are easily captivated by my charismatic and enticing presence.
- I am alluring and mysterious.
- I am powerful.
- I exude confidence everywhere I go.
- I'm ridiculously hot without even trying.
- I can have anybody and whatever I desire.
- People are always enamored by my allure and seductiveness.
- I am the most powerful lady in the world.
- People are amazed by my beauty.
- People are captivated by me because I am a total enigma.
- I am the IT girl.
- I am the quintessential femme fatale.
- I am intimidating.
- I am letting go of every negativity, hate, and self-hatred directed towards me.

- This is my story, and I play the lead role.
- I exude mystery, sensuality, and charm.
- I am my best self.
- I am utterly unaffected by the actions of others.
- At this very moment, my life is fantastic.

Fake it till you make it. Even if you don't believe the things you're speaking right now, you will eventually, and you"ll manifest the ideal femme fatale persona you are meant to be.

We will explore some darker and extremly powerful affirmations later on.

It's an exciting journey if you decide to invest in yourself. Essentially, it means giving in to your wildest fantasies and releasing the person you've always hidden deep within you. It's about giving the dark feminine room to shine and meeting her wants, redirecting your attention to the things that matter, and then sitting back to enjoy the fruits of your labor as your manifestations come to fruition.

At any given time, you have the ability to transform into this version of yourself. Anyone is capable of dominating and manipulating a man. This is all about recognizing your power, establishing a connection with your dark feminine identity, and directing that connection into the reality you are living in now.
The first thing you need to do to regain control is to convince yourself that you already have it.

Chapter Five

The Femme Fatale Seduction

The femme fatale persona is the most dangerous, alluring, and manipulative kind of seductress possible for a woman to embody. To be a successful femme fatale, you must follow four golden principles.

Seduction is about fantasy and idealization.

This section elaborates on these guidelines, which constitute the basis of their worldview with regard to their behavior toward males.

Pay close attention, as we are getting to the really juicy parts.

Principle 1:

A Femme Fatale Never Chases

Men don't want you to know this, yet their greatest pleasure comes from the thrill of the chase. They take great pleasure in the struggle to achieve their goals. This pertains to sexual activity, romantic partnerships, and closeness with a female.

Women should also feel free to experience this; get into relationships rapidly, have one-night encounters, and engage in sexual activity with men shortly after meeting them. There is no need to be ashamed of this.

To exert dominance over a guy, however, you must put these plans on hold and take things slow. The longer he has to wait to get what he wants, the harder he will try to get it.

Those who want to touch a femme fatale, must first gain her trust. She won't accept anything less than concrete evidence of their professed love for her. She establishes limits that she never, ever bends, and if a guy violates them, she promptly gets rid of him.

A woman's natural role is as a receiver. She reverts to her passive ways, giving men the opportunity to earn her respect and admiration. In addition, the dark femme will not settle for anything less than she has earned. She puts guys in their place when necessary, but when he's succeeding, she's sweet, seductive, and sensual. She never goes to extremes or makes herself seem desperate for a guy.

Choosing not to pursue a guy might indicate several different things. It means not making your life revolve around them in any way. This includes **not initiating text conversations** or making advance **plans for a romantic encounter**. In other words, it implies having a choice. All of this forces guys into their **masculine energy** which in turn increases the likelihood that they will pursue you romantically.

I used to insist on going 50/50 on dates. This stemmed from a hyper-independence I developed due to mommy issues. I felt like I would owe them something in return if they'd pay for the whole date. I know it might be challenging to let go of these habits, but we need to take back our feminine power and learn to receive.

I'm a raging feminist and I support every choice and decision women make, but I'm frustrated to see so many women doing housework, paying the bills, taking care of the children and they get cheated on or left for another women that wouldn't even do 1% of that. Serving men is a social condition that was pushed onto women and has always been proven to work against them. What you must understand is that almost everything of what society tell you to do, it's usually the opposite that is going to work in you favor. I want what's best for my queens. And please remember the following statement:

Respect for female strength does not translate into male attraction

Principle 2: A Femme Fatale is Always In Control

Being needy and dependent is the surest method to drive a guy away as quickly as possible. When attempting to win over a guy, it is important to demonstrate that you have a life of your own. You are not reliant on him in any way, and he will never be able to take priority over you in your decisions.

The secret is to emotionally distance yourself from others and love yourself so much that you won't be so readily impressed by anybody else. This is helpful in many facets of life, not just dating.

Principle 3: A Femme Fatale Creates Her Identity for Others

You need to understand and accept that you can be whoever you want to be. In order to be a femme fatale, you don't need to alter your personality completely. You can either:

1. Incorporate some of the traits into your personality

2. Create an alter ego that you switch into when the situation demands it

The importance of this principle is best represented by a lady's narration of her experience with Marylin Monroe. According to her, she had been out for a stroll in New York City with Marilyn because she felt safe in New York City, where she could wear basic clothing and go unnoticed, in contrast to the ogling she received in Hollywood. Then suddenly, she turned to her as they walked along Broadway and asked, "Do you want to see me become her?" The lady answered "Yes" without really understanding what Marilyn meant. Then, she did something that was so subtle that it was nearly magical. And suddenly, traffic came to a halt, and onlookers turned to gaze. Even if nobody had seen her a moment before, everybody seemed to realize that she was Marilyn Monroe.

Marilyn Monroe was a walking example of how having self-assurance and believing in yourself can alter the world around you. It was clear from the moment she said, "do you want to see me become her," that everyone has the potential to turn into a femme fatale at any time. You do not need to undergo significant changes to your look or spend hundreds of dollars on brand-new cosmetic and aesthetic goods.

However, if you change your way of thinking about yourself and begin to perceive yourself as a treasure, others will start to do the same. Men will crumble before you. You won't have to do anything at all, yet you'll still manage to have them all caught up in it. Altering your energy has several beneficial side effects, including increased influence over men. If you love yourself first and foremost, everything else in life will fall into place for you.

Principle 4: A Femme Fatale has Mastered the Art of Detachment

Detachment is one of the most crucial abilities to develop when it comes to seduction since it is one of the most effective techniques. "The condition of being objective and aloof" is one of the definitions of detachment, and this is precisely what you need to be to succeed. It indicates that you are unable to connect with the person.

Being detached enables you to behave rationally and guarantees that your feelings for the target will not taint your seduction. It gives you the ability to view things as they are, rather than how you wish them to be, and it enables you to let other people be who they are without judging them based on their potential.

Keeping your distance from other people causes them to become more reliant on you because, once they see you can get by without their help, they are more likely to appreciate you. However, how do you detach yourself from other people and things?

l Acceptance: Realize that not everything is intended for you and that the things that are meant for you will find you, while the things that are not meant for you will fade away. When you put your happiness in the hands of other people, you put yourself in danger of being affected by the actions and choices that others make.

You are responsible for your happiness. It doesn't matter how much you want something or someone; they might walk out on you anytime, and you can't allow this stuff to break you. It's just the way life is.

2. Release: Figure out how to let go of things that aren't going the way you want them to. Put an end to imposing your will on others. Adopt the philosophy that there is a cause for everything that occurs.

3. Allowance: Give yourself and others permission to be your authentic, unrestrained selves without fear of being judged. Recognize yourself and others in all of their fullness.

Chapter Six

Inflicting Obsession

Alright, here we go. The part you've all been waiting for. I've compiled and curated all the information from various sources, dark feminine gurus and personal experience.

Before beginning the process of seduction or infatuation, it is important to develop a character that embodies the femme fatale archetype and reach a level of ease in which you can completely embrace your dark femininity. You must have faith in who you are and make sure that you are not putting yourself in a situation where you may be hurt for this to be successful.

An obsession is not always healthy, and there are occasions when it may be both hazardous and frightening. Be careful not to go too far unless you want someone to follow you and think about you nonstop with an obsessive focus every second of the day.

At the start of this journey, the first thing to do is to choose your target male persona. Every single guy may be placed into one of these categories, and every man is susceptible to being tricked into obsessed. Before beginning the manipulation process, it is essential to do research, make observations, and understand your target. There is one item that the target lacks in their life, which varies from target to target, and this is the tool that you must use to your advantage.

Male Target Types

The Geek

The word "geek" refers to guys who approach things in a rational manner. They divide every aspect of their life into distinct sections, each of which may be investigated in more depth and are often quite bright.

They often have a "geek" social label attached to them already and have an interest in the sciences, mathematics, and computers. They communicate logically and analytically, seldom allowing their emotions to influence their choices.

How to manipulate him into obsession

The geek's desire to feel superior, owing to their brilliance, puts them in a mental prison, and the lack of excitement and adventure in their life is a direct result of this need. One of two things has to be done if you want to make people fascinated with you. First, you can't challenge their intellectual supremacy by giving the impression that you are smarter than them; doing so would drive them farther away.

To give the impression that you are more knowledgeable about life, you should be lively, impulsive, and full of new encounters and adventures. Act on your impulses without explaining why you are doing what you are doing. You should let them rule you in reasoning and intellect, but you should dominate them and take the lead in matters of the experience of life.

The Innocent

The innocent guy is the most specific target for manipulation. They have a life perspective characterized by openness and empathy for others. They have no preconceived notions about the world and can see the best in everyone. They have a propensity for being rather meek and innocent.

How to manipulate him into obsession

You should make every effort to avoid becoming naive like them. Instead, show them your dark feminine side and the wisdom you've gained from life. Take on the persona of a leader or someone stronger than them. Innocent types are naturally subservient and have a strong sense of their inferiority. Bring them into your world and make them feel like they can't go on without you after you've gotten them to like you and established a rapport with them.

The Cold One

These males are seen as "cold" or "rough" because they display little or no emotions. The cold one is aloof and don't seem to trust anyone unless they prove themselves to him.

They lack vulnerability, often due to their desire to emotionally shield themselves due to previous traumatic experiences, miseducation, or other factors.

The cold male persona requires a lot of effort. Due to the fact that they are exceedingly resistant to having their walls broken down and are quite disconnected, the procedure must be carried out slowly and with utmost care. Never under any circumstances attempt to force a bond between the two of you.

How to manipulate them into obsession

When you get a glimpse of their vulnerability amid their icy demeanor, you have found a doorway into their feelings. Take a mental note of it, and then, later on, utilize that subject to bring down their defenses gradually. Do NOT try any manipulation technique as they're quick to pull away. Earn their trust slowly, let them come to you and they'll slowly find themselves craving your presence more and more.

The Narcissist

Every one of us has had the experience of interacting with a narcissistic male. They are high maintenance, think the world revolves around them, and are self-absorbed to the extreme. They have an unhealthy preoccupation with themselves.

The key to understanding narcissistic men is to understand that they are dissatisfied with themselves and their lives. As a result, they look for validation in every situation they can. As a result, how they might achieve their preoccupation is to stoke the fires of their self-obsession by satisfying their egos.

How to manipulate them into obsession

Do not acknowledge them, congratulate them, or validate their position. Because of their never-ending need for attention, they will always be hungry for more. Rather, challenge them, while trying to challenge their ego, make sure you don't go too far with it. Find a method to strike a balance with it by validating it, taking a step back, and then challenging it again.

The Andrew Tate Wannabe
(sorry, couldn't help myself)

The Andrew Tate fanboys, the alpha male podcasters and the incels that spread misogynistic content – they're all the same type. The controlling, "dominant" ones. This type of men are similar to the Cold One in the sense that you have to "prove" yourself to them, otherwise they will lump you together with the rest of the seemingly "unworthy" females.

These guys have an unquenchable desire to dominate all facets of life, which shows in everything they do. Typically, they have experienced emotions of helplessness and fragility throughout their childhood, which has led to a psychological need for control as an adult.

Typically, these guys attempt to dictate the clothes you wear, the people you associate with, and the activities you participate in throughout your life.

How to manipulate them into obsession

Men who are controlling often feel insecure in their own lives, and as a result, they want to exert their authority over everything to compensate for this. All that is required of you is to give them the impression that they are in charge of the situation even if they are not necessarily in control, and you will be the one covertly directing everything behind the scenes.

The Romantic

Another kind that is simple to captivate is the romantic. These kinds of guys are head over heels for the concept of love.

They want a girlfriend, the commitment, and to stay with you till they die. They want to spend the rest of their lives with you. You'll be able to identify a romantic by their effort in your predicament.

People with this persona often like reading or watching movies in the fantasy romance genre.

How to manipulate the into obsession

Because they see their fixation with you as an expression of love, it is not difficult to convince someone of this kind to become obsessed with you. You have to indulge their fantasies in some way. The tenderness, the romance, and the thrilling experiences all rolled into one.

However, the most important thing you can do in this situation is to avoid developing attachments. This is due to the fact that you will get ice cold just before the finish line, either because they made a mistake or because they got too comfy. They will get obsessed with regaining the nice and lovely side of you that they have become used to because they will miss it.

The Player

These males like playing with other people's feelings, particularly women. They have several partners with the expectation of gaining praise from others, and they believe their behavior is justified when they break up with women who are in love with them. They tend to have a large number of casual encounters and close personal connections, and they continue to keep their choices open. They often engage in flirtatious behavior and are known to tell many crude jokes. They have the mindset that they can never be restrained.

How to manipulate them into obsession

You can never be too serious with this persona, be playful and exhibit a sexy and entertaining side of yourself. It is beneficial to examine their behavior and attempt to infer why they act the way they do.

Once you've identified their vulnerability, you may bring it out to them straightforwardly and enjoy watching their reaction as they realize how accurate you were.

Another strategy for seducing them is to put on an innocent front fully. This is due to the fact that it gives them the impression that they have full power over you, whereas, in reality, you are the one who is pulling the strings behind the scenes.

The Victim

The victims, the unappreciated nice guys, the ones who are always overlooked. Another easy type to manipulate. These guys aren't usually the most attractive and don't have much experience when it comes to women.
They were forced on developing their personalities to compensate for not being conventionally attractive and are usually very empathetic and funny.

How to manipulate them into obsession

Build a connection with them. Give them the attention they so desire and make it exclusive. Focus only on them and make them feel special. Don't inflate their ego too much though. They secretly want to be a player and you know what they say about giving the ugly guy a chance.

What causes obsession?

You have a quality that they want for themselves

You bring out a suppressed version of themselves.

There's a saying that opposites attract. This is what it's referring to.

A good example is the "bad guy" trope. Why does the girl always fall for the bad boys? Because with the bad boy, she 's free of the responsibility of always having to be the "good girl" that she's had to portray her whole life. She gets to be "bad" through him.

Another example is one that often occurs in movies:

The manic pixie dream girl. Who is she? She's the happy, bubbly girl that suddenly appears in the sad boy's life and teaches him that life is worth living and teaches him what love is.

Again, contrast and opposition can be seen. The sad boy is lacking everything that the manic pixie dream girl is displaying. They live through each other.

Benefits of making someone obsessed with you

Why would you want someone obsessed over you? Well let me finish my story from high school. Sure, guys were asking me out and were drawn to me as I had unconsciously cultivated an aura of mystery. But I had chosen the worst, cruelest narcissist that used every manipulation technique to coerce me into doing his bidding. And I tried to fight back and match the energy but I was already emotionally attached. In college after leaving my hometown and breaking up with him for good, he had conveniently changed.

I was already detached but I wasn't going to let it slide. I learned these techniques and got him infatuated with me. Then I destroyed him. To this day he still tries to desperately reach out and texts me constantly even though I don't even bother responding. He's been telling people that I was his first girlfriend and no one compare to me.

These techniques also made me "the one who got away" for all of my ex boyfriends that I lost interest in.

Another reason is that obsession makes men weak and compliant. And I do enjoy feeling powerful and in control.

It's important that even if you don't plan to use them, to at least know you have the option and the knowledge to do so. Remember, **a Femme Fatale** isn't born, **she's made.**

The Steps Towards Inflicting Obsession

Alright my devilish gals, let's get right into it. The various kinds of male persona targets serve as the primary building blocks for the traps you place. You may start using the following tactics after determining your target.

Choose a target: Make sure that when you choose a target, you choose someone you've already had the opportunity to watch for a period of time. Before taking action, ensure you have a basic grasp of their personality. To what kinds of women do they typically gravitate their attention? Which sort of goal do they most closely reflect? How straightforward will the act of seduction be? Try to get a sense of who they are by listening to how other people describe them but avoid asking too many questions to avoid arousing suspicion. Make sure you have identified the specific segment of the target market they belong to and that you are aware of how to appeal to them.

Command their attention: When attempting to capture the attention of a target, it is essential to have an open mindset and use inviting body language. Although the dark feminine lady has the potential to be menacing, when she is attempting to attract the attention of a target, she remains calm and puts on a big grin.

Being distinct and noticeable is the most effective method for determining whether or not a target is interested in you. This would come easily to you, given your status as a femme fatale. You have an air of intrigue, seduction, and inaccessibility about you, yet at the same time, you are gregarious, charming, and sociable. You are a living example of juxtaposition.

Feelings have a significant role in the formation of good memories. Do you want to be remembered by someone? Be courageous and look them square in the eyes while you're doing it. Speak your mind honestly, and share discrete aspects of who you are with another person to make them feel more important.

Develop your charm: This is an essential phase in the process of seduction since it is what starts to break down their defenses and barriers. Although the femme fatale is very sexual and flirtatious, you shouldn't try to hide your sexual allure, but you also shouldn't engage in any flirtation with them at this point. This guarantees they cannot determine your goal, allowing you to maintain an air of mystery and keep people guessing about what you are up to.

Create a friendship: This is when their resistance starts to weaken. First you must start to **vibe** with them. Vibing is generally an upbeat conversation with rapid changes of topics and pace, some deeper-dives, and snippets of important information about oneself. The next step is making them **open up to you**. You do this by **actively listening** to him. Robert Greene said that people are like open books, most of them love talking about themselves. This is 100% true. When you listen to him, **display excitement** and **curiosity** and **do not judge**. Do not try to force a bond if you're not feeling it right away, have patience and let it occur naturally.

Sell the fantasy

The devil is in the details and the details are what will differentiate you from the masses. People are dying to fantasize about someone.

This is straightforward, yet it is not simple. Make sure you are entirely comfortable with your dark femininity and sensuality before going on to with this step.
It is important you believe that you believe you are the ideal, the treasure to strive towards. When others see you believing something and demonstrating that belief, their imaginations will go wild with concepts.

How you conduct yourself directly reflects how others will regard you. You have to be what you want others to think of you as.

Blur the borders between fear and optimism.

The heart of desire is comprised of both pain and pleasure. Obsession thrives on ambiguous cues and ambiguity, as we have shown before; this much is certain. It is a breeding ground for excessive thinking, and every time you switch between different feelings, you sustain an intense and compulsive loop between yourself and the goal.

So how do you do this? The first step in creating hope is to show that you are interested and attractive, but you should never affirm this verbally. Be sensual and seductive, but avoid giving them an excessive amount of your attention. Never let anybody know your true objectives.

Use the rollercoaster effect

As Robert Green said "the lowers the lows, the higher the highs".

The rollercoaster effect is basically creating anxiety and pain followed by an intense release of tension and pleasure. For example: ghosting them or disappearing out of nowhere – in this timeframe they will inevitably think of you, worry, wonder what you might be doing.

Followed by coming back and giving them a plausible explanation. This will create the need for consistency and attachment. Don't do it too often though!

This is the feature I've embodied in all my past relationships and I've been "the one that got away" for all of my exes. With this trick I've actually managed to make two men believe I was The One for them. And they were in the same friend group. Obsession is so strong that it overtakes reason.

The main feature is making **him feel exclusive**. You have so many options, but you chose him because you've never felt this way about anyone before. Maybe you've had other love interests before, but nothing compares to this. You weren't even genuinely interested in the other guys. You barely even remember them.
You get the point.
If you do this right, he'll remember you forever.

This step is to be done when the relationship feels most intense and passionate.

Exude exclusivity

Not only you should make him feel
exclusive, but you must also be
exclusive yourself. Mystery and
exclusivity go hand in hand so if you
already master the aura of mystery,
being exclusive should be easy. Be
selective of who you spend your time
with and how you spend it. This all
contributes to the image you're trying
to create and they will want you even
more.

Silence tratment

After a time in which things are going well, and they have become too comfortable, it is best to take away this comfort they've gathered from being with you.

Pull back and deprive him of what he knows and inflict confusion. The best method to use is the silent treatment.

Silence is powerful can can effectivly be used in two situations:

- He does something that would normally upset you, so instead of throwing a tantrum you act cold and go silent. After he insists a couple of times, you can tell him how his behavior irritated you

- He got too comfortable and his behavior shows it. Going silent will force him to be back on his best behavior.

Conceal your intentions

Make them do whatever you want by being sweet and charming.
Never try to coerce them into doing something. People are skeptical as it is and coercing them into doing something is not going to work. So you want to point out the benefit they get out of doing something. They won't do it because you say so, you're just looking out for them and want what's best.
You get more bees with honey.

Combatting resistance

People love being seduced. So if you hit a wall, don't panic – it's perfectly normal. There are two main reasons why people:

-You're not his type
-He's scared of getting hurt

We will need to break his resistance by creating the most powerful fantasy there is. The **forbidden romance.**

Creating a forbidden romance will make him desperately crave you. He'll want you 10x time more.

Play on their insecurities

Observe them and learn what their insecurities are. They won't say what they're insecure about, we have to deduce this from their actions and body language.

If they get **defensive** about a certain topic or aspect of themselves and feel the need to o**ver explain**, that's what they're most likely insecure about. Now we'll create the **cycle of validation** in which we tease them about their insecurity and we cover it up immediately saying it's a joke.

For instance if they're insecure about you leave them, make a playful joke saying you'll leave him. Then immediately give the them relief of pleasure (in this case hope) reassuring them that will never happen.

Crushing your target

Leave them high and dry

The ultimate step into making them obsessed with you forever and the the cruelest revenge tactic.

After about a year, when you have gotten everything you wanted out of him, give him a last taste of his desires and of showcase your future with him one more time. Make him see how great and amazing you are.

When he's going to think he finally got you, abruptly **cut contact** with him with no explanation.

Dissappear, leave him at his happiest.

He's going to c**rave closure** and you will forever represent the road not taken, the mysterious unknown, the embodiment of an alternative life.

You will be on of his mind forever and he will always be mesmerized by you.

Extra

Powerful Manifestations

If you follow me on Tiktok, you
might know that I am currently
dwelling almost entirely in my
dark energy. Like 99%.
I will show you some the
affirmations I use. Be aware, as
they're very dark and very
powerful.
You can use them too, but make
sure they come from a good place.
As much as you can at least.

- This is my world and everyone else is just existing in it.
- I am the absolute best.
- No one compare to my beauty.
- Everyone I meet becomes obsessed with me.
- Every man I meet adores me.
- My energy is addictive
- My personality is sexy and seductive
- People are mesmerized by me
- My aura is hypnotic
- I am the most powerful woman in the world
- I am a dangerous seductress
- I adore every part of myself
- I am better than anyone else and they know it
- Everyone is intimidated by me

Manifestation

Look, I was skeptical at the beginning.
I thought it was just a trend or some means to create content.
That was until I actually tried it. It worked.
And it wasn't something that was likely to happen.
What were the odds that a guy whom I hadn't spoken to in 3 years would contact me and tell me he still had feeling for me?
I mean, I know my seduction skills are on point, but what were the odds that he confessed it right after three days of me manifesting it.
I was shocked for a few minutes, the I started laughing uncontrollably. It scared me a bit, not gonna lie.

Along with affirmations, manifesting is a quick way to get the results you want. You're probably familiar with this method, but I'm going to list it as it actually works.

You migh've heared of it by now, it's called the **whisper method.**

Here's how you do it:

Close your eyes and envision yourself walking into a room. In that room, you see the person you want something from. They're standing still and they don't acknowledge or see you. You're almost like a spirit.

Go up to them and whisper three times in their ear what you want them to do. It can be something like "Text me" or "You're in love with me".

Similar to affirmations, but you address them to someone.

After you've said it three times, envision yourself kissing their forehead and walk away. The kiss should feel like you sealed the deal.

Now open your eyes and believe you have now entered a reality where that person is going to do what you desire. Believe it with your whole heart, as it will happen. Do this around two times per day until you get the result.

I only did it once and got the result after three days. But I knew it was going to happen.

Maybe I'm really good at manifesting. Either way, I will manifest that all the queens who read this book will be the most powerful and seductive women to ever walk this earth. And all of them will be living their dreamlife very soon.

Golden Tips on the First Date

I want to share a few quick golden tips for the first date. Every single tip will have a psychological effect on your date. You'll have them mesmerized if you follow these.

Tip #1:

On for the first date, do what most smart women do: pretend you can't find him and let him come to you while you look around, walk or check your phone. That dynamic starts from the smallest detail: who's looking at whom.

Tip #2

Create the goddess effect by wearing golden jewelry. Some small golden hoops or a bracelet will sufice. Gold leaves the strongest psychological effect, as it is linked with luxury and wealth. It will indicate your high value.

Tip #3

Go for the following outfits:

- a little black dress and black heels for dinner dates
- a white item of clothing for daytime dates

Use the upper-lower contrast to stay classy and not reveal too much.

Tip #4

Red nails are mandatory! Look up the red nails theory. For make-up, make sure you have a red or pink lipstick on.

Conclusion

These techniques will help you become a skilled manipulator and a fearless maneater.

Take your time and trust the process and always remember who you are and always be aware of the powers you possess.

I love you all and wish you good luck on your journey.

For more questions you can find me at femmefataleguide@gmail.com

My TikTok is @darkdivinefeminine

See you soon.

Yours sincerely,
DarkDivineFeminine

Printed in Great Britain
by Amazon

37731285R00069